First published in 2009
by Evans Brothers Limited
2A Portman Mansions
Chiltern Street
London W1U 6NR
UK

Printed in Dubai

British Library Cataloguing in Publication Data
Phillips, Dee.
   Dare. -- (Right now)
   1. Graphic novels. 2. Young adult fiction.
   I. Title II. Series
   741.5-dc22
   ISBN-13: 9780237539566

Developed & Created by Ruby Tuesday Books Ltd

Project Director – Ruth Owen
Head of Design – Elaine Wilkinson
Designer – Elaine Wilkinson
Editor – Frances Ridley
Consultant – Lorraine Petersen, Chief Executive of NASEN

© Ruby Tuesday Books Limited 2009

ACKNOWLEDGEMENTS

With thanks to Lorraine Petersen, Chief Executive of NASEN for her help in the development and creation of these books.

Images courtesy of Shutterstock; **page 27** Alamy; **page 22** Superstock

While every effort has been made to secure permission to use copyright material, the publishers apologise for any errors or omissions in the above list and would be grateful for notification of any corrections to be included in subsequent editions.

It's just an old, empty house.
I don't believe in ghosts.
That's why I took the dare.

ONE MOMENT CAN CHANGE YOUR LIFE FOREVER

It's dark inside the house.
I shine my torch around.
What a place!

OK. I can do this.
It's just a house – an old,
empty house.

I don't believe in ghosts.
That's why I took the dare.

Tonight, I will sleep in this house.

ALONE.

The dare was Jo and Emma's idea.
They don't think I can do it.
Jo and Emma believe in the ghost.
The ghost of the woman who died in
this house.

I shine my torch around.
There are lots of rooms.
I try some of the doors
but they are locked.

Suddenly, I hear a voice.

Please...

I listen. I look behind me.
Nothing.

I shine my torch up
the stairs.

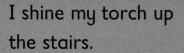

The hairs on the back
of my neck stand up.
I'm hearing things.
This old, empty house
is messing with
my head.

Upstairs there are more locked doors.

Only one door opens.
I step into the room.
Suddenly, I can't breathe.
My mouth is filled with...

...COBWEBS!

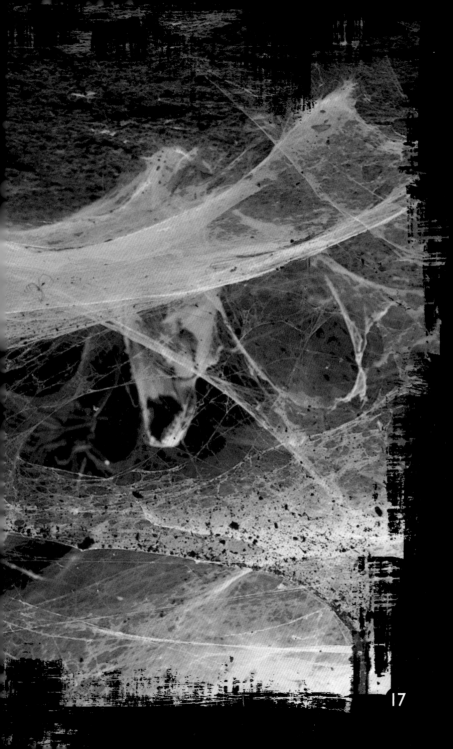

My heart is thumping.
I shine my torch around the room.
Was this a little girl's bedroom?

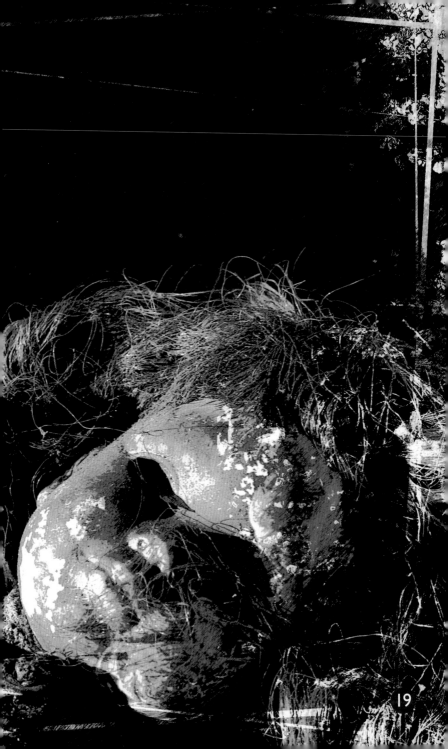

Maybe it was a woman's bedroom?

Then I think of Jo and Emma's story.

A little girl locked up by her father.
Locked up in a room for many, many years.
Then left to die.

There is an old, dusty bed.
I guess I could sleep here.
I put my sleeping bag on
the bed.

I look at my watch.
It's midnight.
I turn off my torch to
save the power.

Please...
Don't leave me.
Take me with you.

Am I dreaming?
Is someone there?

I switch on the torch.

Yuck!

It's just a rat.

I shiver.
This place is messing
with my head.

I get out of bed.
I can't sleep with a rat!
I have to find another room.

27

I try to open the door, but...

...it won't open!

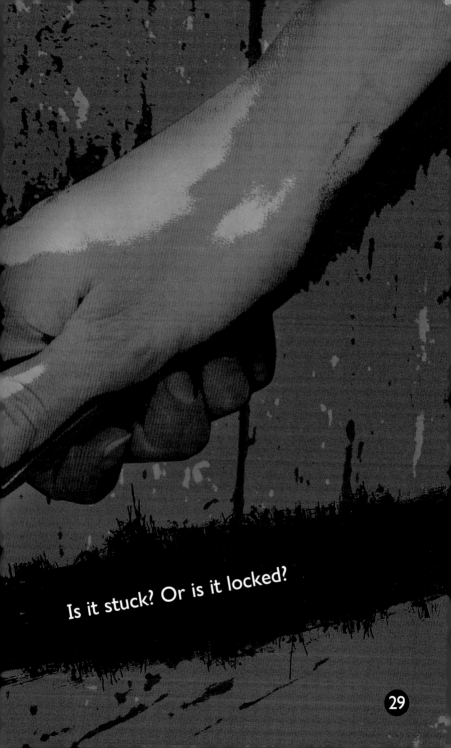

Is it stuck? Or is it locked?

That's when I see the marks.

Marks on the back of
the door.
Is it a hand?

OK. Don't get freaked out.
The door is just stuck.

I get back into my
sleeping bag. It's 3 am.
It will soon be morning.

Take me with you.

I'm your friend now...

...forever.

Did I fall asleep again?

I shine my torch around the room.
Nothing.
Nobody.

It's 5 am.
It will soon be morning.

I wake up and shiver.
It's light outside.

I try the door –
it opens first time!
I did it. It's over.
Now, let's get out
of here!

I open the front door of the house.
The crowd cheers!
I hear the words...

"You did it Lauren. You've won this week's **DARE**."

I see Jo and Emma cheering in the crowd.

DARE is their favourite TV show. Every week, somebody spends the night in a spooky place.

Of course, it's all fake.

A big screen shows my
night in the house.

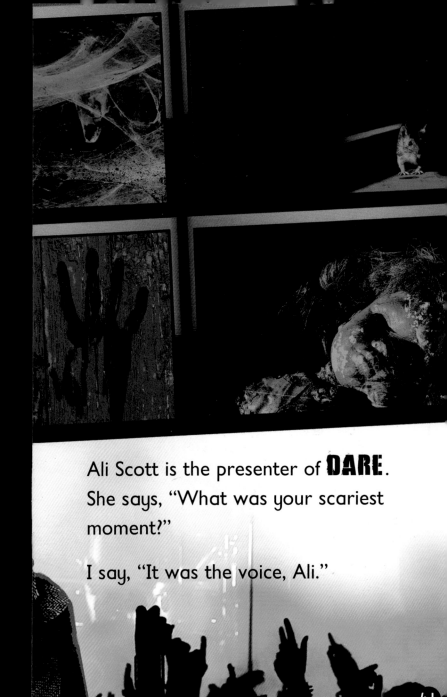

Ali Scott is the presenter of **DARE**.
She says, "What was your scariest
moment?"

I say, "It was the voice, Ali."

Ali smiles and nods.
She looks at her notes.
She stops smiling.
She checks her notes again.

Ali says, "Lauren, there
wasn't any voice."

I shiver.

Take me with you.
I'm your friend now...

...forever.

43

DARE - WHAT'S NEXT?

HAUNTED HOUSE
ON YOUR OWN

Invent a game based on a night in a haunted house.

- It could be a board game or a computer game.
- You can use events from the DARE story, or your own ideas.

- It could be a board game in which the players solve problems using clues. For example, find a door that isn't locked.
- A computer game could have different levels.

WHAT SCARES YOU?
WITH A PARTNER

Everyone is scared of different things.

- Are you scared of spooky places, such as graveyards? Maybe you have a fear of heights, or snakes? With your partner discuss what scares you.
- What would YOU or your partner do for a dare? Take it in turn to think up dares. Be honest about whether you would take the dare or not.

BELiEVERS?
IN A GROUP

Hold a group debate on this subject: *"Ghosts exist in the real world."*

• Everyone decides which side they are on – for or against.

• Each side prepares its argument. Collect as much evidence as you can!

• Hold the debate and take a vote at the end. Which side won?

GHOST STORIES
ON YOUR OWN / WITH A PARTNER / IN A GROUP

Tell a ghost story! It could be based on real events, or make up a story of your own. Make it as creepy as possible. You could:

• Record yourself telling the story.
• Tell your story to a partner.
• Swap stories at a "ghost story" session.

IF YOU ENJOYED
THIS BOOK,
TRY THESE OTHER
RiGHT NOW!
BOOKS.

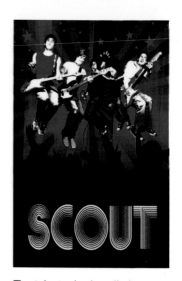

Tonight is the band's big chance. Tonight, a record company scout is at their gig!

Tonight, Vicky must make a choice. Stay in London with her boyfriend Chris. Or start a new life in Australia.

Dan sees the red car. The keys are inside. Dan says to Andy, Sam and Jess, "Want to go for a drive?"

It's Saturday night.
Two angry guys. Two knives.
There's going to be a fight.

Sophie hates this new town.
She misses her friends.
There's nowhere to skate!

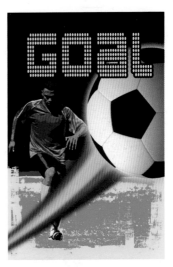

Ed's platoon is under attack.
Another soldier is in danger.
Ed must risk his own life to
save him.

Today is Carl's trial with
City. There's just one place
up for grabs. But today,
everything is going wrong!